This notebook belongs to:

____

Published by Neaterstuff Publishing

Made in the USA
Middletown, DE
12 October 2023

40675781R00068